♥ Table of contents ♥

Panel 1

There are 3 things you can do to a file

↓ read ↓ write ↓ execute

Panel 2

ls -l file.txt shows you permissions. Here's how to interpret the output:

rw-   rw-   r--   bork staff

bork (user) can read & write

staff (group) can read & write

ANYONE can read

Panel 3

File permissions are 12 bits

setuid setgid
↓   ↓   user   group   all
000   110   110   100
sticky   rwx   rwx   rwx

For files:
    r = can read
    w = can write
    x = can execute
For directories, it's approximately:
    r = can list files
    w = can create files
    x = can cd into & access files

Panel 4

110 in binary is 6

So rw-   r--   r--
  = 110   100   100
  = 6   4   4

chmod 644 file.txt means change the permissions to:

rw- r-- r--

Simple!

Panel 5

setuid affects executables

$ls -l /bin/ping

rws r-x r-x root root
↑
this means ping always runs as root

setgid does 3 different unrelated things for executables, directories, and regular files.

unix! why?!

it's a long story

unix

an amazing directory: /proc

Every process on Linux has a PID (process ID) like 42.

In /proc/42, there's a lot of VERY USEFUL information about process 42.

/proc/PID/cmdline

command line arguments the process was started with

/proc/PID/exe

symlink to the process's binary. magic: works even if the binary has been deleted!

/proc/PID/environ

all of the process's environment variables

/proc/PID/status

Is the program running or asleep? How much memory is it using? And much more!

/proc/PID/fd

Directory with every file the process has open!

Run $ ls -l /proc/42/fd to see the list of files for process 42.

These symlinks are also magic & you can use them to recover deleted files ♥

/proc/PID/stack

The kernel's current stack for the process. Useful if it's stuck in a system call.

/proc/PID/maps

List of process's memory maps. Shared libraries, heap, anonymous maps, etc.

and ·more·

Look at

man proc

for more information!

system calls

The Linux kernel has code to do a lot of things

- read from a hard drive
- make network connections
- create new process
- kill process
- change file permissions
- keyboard drivers

your program doesn't know how to do those things

> TCP? dude I have no idea how that works.

> NO, I do not know how the ext4 filesystem is implemented. I just want to read some files!

programs ask Linux to do work for them using ≡system calls≡

program: > please write to this file

〈switch to running kernel code〉

> done! I wrote 1097 bytes! — Linux

〈program resumes〉

every program uses system calls

Python program: > I use the 'open' syscall to open files

Java program: > me too!

> me three! — C program

and every system call has a number
(e.g. chmod is #90 on x86-64)

So what's actually going on when you change a file's permissions is:

program: > run syscall #90 with these arguments

> ok! — Linux

you can see which system calls a program is using with {strace}

$ strace ls /tmp

will show you every system call 'ls' uses! it's really fun!

⚠ strace has high overhead so don't run it on your production database

signals

If you've ever used ⚡kill⚡ you've used signals

DIE!!!

okay

process

the Linux kernel sends processes signals in lots of situations

- your child terminated
- that pipe is closed
- illegal instruction
- the timer you set expired
- Segmentation fault

you can send signals yourself with the kill system call or command

SIGINT	Ctrl-C	various levels of "die"
SIGTERM	kill	
SIGKILL	kill -9	

SIGHUP kill -HUP

often interpreted as "reload config", e.g. by nginx

Every signal has a default action, which is one of:

- ☺ ignore
- 😣 kill process
- 😣≈ kill process AND make core dump file
- 😐 stop process
- 😊 resume process

Your program can set custom handlers for almost any signal

SIGTERM (terminate)

okay! I'll clean up and then exit!

process

exceptions: SIGSTOP & SIGKILL can't be ignored

got → SIGKILLed

signals can be hard to handle correctly since they can happen at ANY time

process handling a signal

SURPRISE! another signal!

file descriptors

Panel 1

Unix systems use integers to track open files

process → "Open foo.txt"

kernel → "okay! that's file #7 for you."

these integers are called file descriptors

Panel 2

lsof (list open files) will show you a process's open files

```
$ lsof -p 4242     ← PID we're interested in
FD   NAME
0    /dev/pts/tty1
1    /dev/pts/tty1
2    pipe:29174
3    /home/bork/awesome.txt
5    /tmp/
```

FD is for file descriptor

Panel 3

file descriptors can refer to:
→ files on disk
→ pipes
→ sockets (network connections)
→ terminals (like xterm)
→ devices (your speaker! /dev/null!)
→ LOTS MORE (eventfd, inotify, signalfd, epoll, etc.)

"not EVERYTHING on Unix is a file, but lots of things are"

Panel 4

When you read or write to a file/pipe/network connection you do that using a file descriptor

"connect to google.com"

OS → "ok! fd is 5!"

"write GET / HTTP/1.1 to fd #5"

OS → "done!"

Panel 5

Let's see how some simple Python code works under the hood:

Python:
```
f = open("file.txt")
f.readlines()
```

Behind the scenes:

Python program → "open file.txt"

OS → "ok! fd is 4"

Python program → "read from file #4"

OS → "here are the contents!"

Panel 6

(almost) every process has 3 standard FDs:

stdin → 0
stdout → 1
stderr → 2

"read from stdin"
means
"read from the file descriptor 0"

could be a pipe or file or terminal

pipes

Sometimes you want to send the <u>output</u> of one process to the <u>input</u> of another

$$ \$ \ ls \ | \ wc \ -l $$

$$ 53 $$

↖ 53 files !

---

a <u>pipe</u> is a pair of 2 magical file descriptors

① pipe input **IN → OUT** ② pipe output

↗ls   ↗wc
stdin **IN → OUT** stdout
              pipe

When ls does write(**IN**, "hi"),

wc can read it!
read(**OUT**)
→ "hi"

Pipes are one way. →
You can't write to **OUT**.

Linux creates a <u>buffer</u> for each pipe.

ls ↘   ↗ wc
      buffer
IN | data waiting to be read | **OUT**

If data gets written to the pipe faster than it's read, the buffer will fill up. **IN** ▐▌▌▌▌▌ **OUT**

When the buffer is full, writes to **IN** will block (wait) until the reader reads. This is normal & ok ☺

---

what if your target process dies?

↗ls   ↗wc
  ☓☓   ☹

If wc dies, the pipe will close and ls will be sent SIGPIPE. By default, SIGPIPE terminates your process.

---

named pipes

$ mkfifo my-pipe

This lets 2 unrelated processes communicate through a pipe !

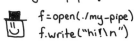 f=open(./my-pipe)
f.write("hi!\n")

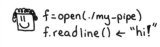 f=open(./my-pipe)
f.readline() ← "hi!"

Panel 1:

networking protocols are complicated

TCP/IP Illustrated Volume 1

Stevens

600 pages

what if I just want to download a cat picture?

Panel 2:

Unix systems have an API called the "socket API" that makes it easier to make network connections

Unix

you don't need to know how TCP works. I'll take care of it!

Panel 3:

here's what getting a cat picture with the socket API looks like:

① Create a socket

fd = socket(AF_INET, SOCK_STREAM, ...)

② Connect to an IP/port

Connect(fd, 12.13.14.15:80)

③ Make a request

write(fd, "GET /cat.png HTTP/1.1 ...")

④ Read the response

cat_picture = read(fd ...)

Panel 4:

Every HTTP library uses sockets under the hood

$ curl awesome.com → sockets

Python: requests.get("yay.us") → sockets

oh, cool, I could write an HTTP library too if I wanted.* Neat!

* SO MANY edge cases though!

Panel 5:

AF_INET? What's that?

AF_INET means basically "internet socket": it lets you connect to other computers on the internet using their IP address.

The main alternative is AF_UNIX ("unix domain socket") for connecting to programs on the same computer.

Panel 6:

3 kinds of internet (AF_INET) sockets:

SOCK_STREAM = TCP

curl uses this

SOCK_DGRAM = UDP

dig (DNS) uses this

SOCK_RAW = just let me send IP packets. I will implement my own protocol.

ping uses this

unix domain sockets are files.

$ file mysock.sock
socket

the file's permissions determine who can send data to the socket.

they let 2 programs on the same computer communicate.

Docker uses Unix domain sockets, for example!

process → GET /container ← HTTP request

Here you go! → 🐳 docker

There are 2 kinds of unix domain sockets:

stream → like TCP! Lets you send a continuous stream of bytes.

datagram → like UDP! Lets you send discrete chunks of data

advantage 1

Lets you use file permissions to restrict access to HTTP/database services!

chmod 600 secret.sock

This is why Docker uses a unix domain socket. 🔒

process — run evil container — permission denied — Linux

advantage 2

UDP sockets aren't always reliable (even on the same computer).
unix domain datagram sockets <u>are</u> reliable! And they won't reorder packets!

process — I can send data and I know it'll arrive

advantage 3

You can send a file descriptor over a unix domain socket.
Useful when handling untrusted input files!

process — here's a file I downloaded from sketchy.com — video decoder

sandboxed process

what's in a {process}?

PID

process #129 reporting for duty!

USER and GROUP

Who are you running as?

julia!

ENVIRONMENT VARIABLES

like PATH! you can set them with:

$ env A=val ./program

SIGNAL HANDLERS

I ignore SIGTERM!

I shut down safely!

WORKING DIRECTORY

Relative paths (./blah) are relative to the working directory! chdir changes it.

PARENT PID

PID 1 (init) is everyone's ancestor

PID 147

PID 129

COMMAND LINE ARGUMENTS

See them in

/proc/PID/cmdline

OPEN FILES

Every open file has an offset.

I've read 8000 bytes of that one

MEMORY

heap! stack!
shared libraries!
the program's binary!
mmaped files!

THREADS

sometimes one
sometimes LOTS

CAPABILITIES

I have CAP_PTRACE

well I have CAP_SYS_ADMIN

NAMESPACES

I'm in the host network namespace

I have my own namespace!

container process

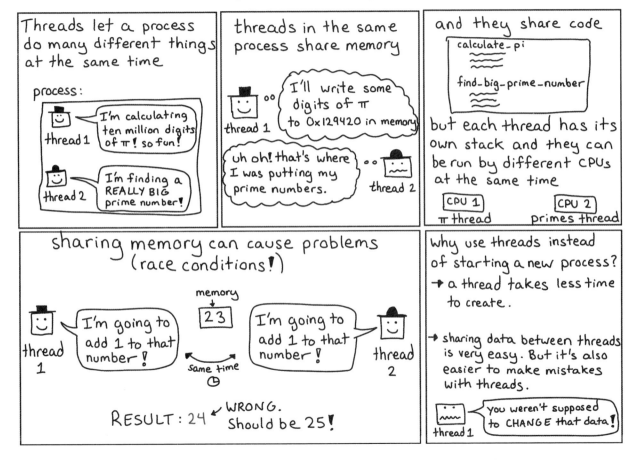

floating point

a double is 64 bits

sign exponent fraction

10011011 10011011 10011011 10011011
10011011 10011011 10011011 10011011

$$\pm 2^{E-1023} \times 1.\text{frac}$$

That means there are 2^{64} doubles.
The biggest one is about

$$2^{1023}$$

weird double arithmetic

$$2^{52} + 0.2 = 2^{52}$$

← (the next number after 2^{52} is $2^{52}+1$)

$$1 + \frac{1}{2^{54}} = 1$$

← (the next number after 1 is $1 + \frac{1}{2^{52}}$)

$$2^{2000} = \text{infinity}$$

← infinity is a double

$$\text{infinity} - \text{infinity} = \text{nan}$$

← nan = "not a number"

---

doubles get farther apart as they get bigger

between 2^n and 2^{n+1} there are always 2^{52} doubles, evenly spaced.

that means the next double after 2^{60} is $2^{60}+64$ ↖ $\frac{2^{60}}{2^{52}}$

Javascript only has doubles (no integers!)

> 2 ** 53
9007199254740992

> 2 ** 53 + 1
9007199254740992

↗ same number! uh oh!

---

doubles are scary and their arithmetic is weird!

they're very logical! just understand how they work and don't use integers over 2^{53} in Javascript ♥

file buffering

I printed some text but it didn't appear on the screen. why??

time to learn about flushing!

On Linux, you write to files & terminals with the system call

♥ write ♥

process: please write "I ♥ cats" to file #1 (stdout)

Linux: okay!

I/O libraries don't always call write when you print.

`printf("I ♥ cats");`

printf: I'll wait for a newline before actually writing

This is called buffering and it helps save on syscalls.

---

3 kinds of buffering
(defaults vary by library)

① None. This is the default for stderr.

② Line buffering. (write after newline). The default for terminals.

③ "full" buffering. (write in big c unks) The default for files and pipes.

---

flushing

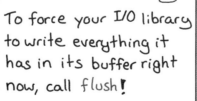

To force your I/O library to write everything it has in its buffer right now, call flush!

stdio: I'll call write right away!!

---

when it's useful to flush

→ when writing an interactive prompt!

Python example:
`print("password: ", flush=True)`

→ when you're writing to a pipe/socket

program: no seriously, actually write to that pipe please

memory allocation

your program has memory

▭	10MB	program binary
▭	3MB	stack
▭	587MB	heap

↑
the heap is what your allocator manages

your memory allocator (malloc) is responsible for 2 things.

THING 1: keep track of what memory is used/free.

587 MB   ▨ used   ☐ free

THING 2: Ask the OS for more memory!

▨ used   ☐ free

malloc oo oh no! I'm being asked for 40 MB and I don't have it.

malloc can I have 60 MB more?

here you go! OS

your memory allocator's interface

malloc (size_t size)
allocate size bytes of memory & return a pointer to it.

free (void* pointer)
mark the memory as unused (and maybe give back to the OS).

realloc(void* pointer, size_t size)
ask for more/less memory for pointer.

calloc (size_t members, size_t size)
allocate array + initialize to 0.

malloc tries to fill in unused space when you ask for memory

your code can I have 512 bytes of memory?

YES! malloc

your new memory ♥

malloc isn't ≡magic≡!
it's just a function!

you can always:

→ use a different malloc library like jemalloc or tcmalloc (easy!)

→ implement your own malloc (harder)

your computer has physical memory

♡ memory ♡
8GB 204-PIN SODIMM DDR3 CE ⓛ

---

physical memory has addresses, like

0 - 8GB

but when your program references an address like 0x 5c69a2a2,

that's not a physical memory address! It's a virtual address.

---

every program has its own virtual address space

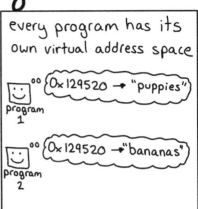

program 1 — Ox 129520 → "puppies"

program 2 — Ox 129520 → "bananas"

Linux keeps a mapping from virtual memory pages to physical memory pages called the page table

a "page" is a 4kb* chunk of memory   *or sometimes bigger

PID	virtual addr	physical addr
1971	0x 20000	0x 192000
2310	0x 20000	0x 228000
2310	0x 21000	0x 9788000

---

when your program accesses a virtual address

CPU: I'm accessing 0x 21000

MMU "memory management unit" hardware: I'll look that up in the page table and then access the right physical address

---

every time you switch which process is running, Linux needs to switch the page table

Linux: here's the address of process 2950's page table

MMU: thanks, I'll use that now!

shared libraries

Most programs on Linux use a bunch of C libraries.

some popular libraries:

openssl (for SSL!)

sqlite (embedded db!)

lib pcre (regular expressions!)

zlib (gzip!)

libstdc++ (C++ standard library!)

There are 2 ways to use any library:

① Link it into your binary

| your code | zlib | sqlite |

big binary with lots of things!

② Use separate shared libraries

| your code | ← all different
| zlib | sqlite | ↙ files

Programs like this

| your code | zlib | sqlite |

are called "statically linked"

and programs like this

| your code | | zlib | | sqlite |

are called "dynamically linked"

---

how can I tell what shared libraries a program is using?

ldd!!

```
$ ldd /usr/bin/curl
   libz.so.1 => /lib/x86-64...
   libresolv.so.2 => ...
   libc.so.6 => ...
   + 34 more ☺
```

I got a "library not found" error when running my binary ?!

If you know where the library is, try setting the LD_LIBRARY_PATH environment variable

LD_LIBRARY_PATH tells me where to look!

dynamic linker

Where the dynamic linker looks

① DT_RPATH in your executable

② LD_LIBRARY_PATH

③ DT_RUNPATH in executable

④ /etc/ld.so.cache (run ldconfig -p to see contents)

⑤ /lib , /usr/lib

copy on write

On Linux, you start new processes using the fork() or clone() system call.

calling fork creates a child process that's a copy of the caller

parent   child

---

the cloned process has EXACTLY the same memory.

→ same heap

→ same stack

→ same memory maps

if the parent has 3GB of memory, the child will too.

---

copying all that memory every time we fork would be slow and a waste of RAM

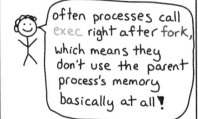

often processes call exec right after fork, which means they don't use the parent process's memory basically at all!

---

so Linux lets them share physical RAM and only copies the memory when one of them tries to write

process — I'd like to change that memory

okay! I'll make you your own copy! — Linux

Linux does this by giving both the processes identical page tables.

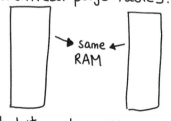

same RAM

but it marks every page as read only.

When a process tries to write to a shared memory address:

① there's a page fault

② Linux makes a copy of the page & updates the page table

③ the process continues, blissfully ignorant

process oo — It's just like I have my own copy

page faults

every Linux process has a page table

★ page table ★

virtual memory address	physical memory address
0x19723000	0x1422000
0x19724000	0x1423000
0x1524000	not in memory
0x1844000	0x4a000 read only

---

some pages are marked as either

★ read only

★ not resident in memory

when you try to access a page that's marked "not resident in memory", it triggers a ! page fault !

---

what happens during a page fault?

→ the MMU sends an interrupt

→ your program stops running

→ Linux kernel code to handle the page fault runs

Linux: I'll fix the problem and let your program keep running

---

"not resident in memory" usually means the data is on disk!

virtual memory

↙ in RAM   ↘ on disk

Having some virtual memory that is actually on disk is how swap and mmap work.

---

how swap works

① run out of RAM
RAM→
disk→

② Linux saves some RAM data to disk
RAM→
disk→

③ mark those pages as "not resident in memory" in the page table   not resident
virtual memory
RAM

④ When a program tries to access the memory, there's a ! page fault !

⑤ Linux: time to move some data back to RAM!
virtual memory
RAM

⑥ if this happens a lot, your program gets VERY SLOW
I'm always waiting for data to be moved in & out of RAM

mmap

What's mmap for?

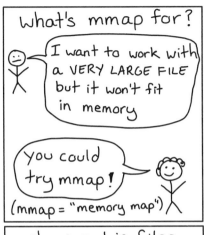

"I want to work with a VERY LARGE FILE but it won't fit in memory"

"You could try mmap!"

(mmap = "memory map")

load files lazily with mmap

When you mmap a file, it gets **mapped** into your program's **memory**.

2TB file → [ ] ← 2TB of virtual memory

but nothing is ACTUALLY read into RAM until you try to access the memory.
(how it works: page faults!)

how to mmap in Python

```
import mmap
f= open ("HUGE.txt")
mm= mmap.mmap (f.fileno(), 0)
```
↖ this won't read the file from disk! Finishes ~instantly.

```
print (mm[-1000:])
```
↑ this will read only the last 1000 bytes!

sharing big files with mmap

☺ ☺ ☺ "we all want to read the same file!"

"no problem!" → mmap

Even if 10 processes mmap a file, it will only be read into memory ♥once♥

dynamic linking uses mmap

☺ program — "I need to use libc.so.6"

C standard library

"you too eh? no problem. I always mmap, so that file is probably loaded into memory already."

[ld] dynamic linker

anonymous memory maps

→ not from a file (memory set to 0 by default)

→ with MAP_SHARED, you can use them to share memory with a subprocess!

man page sections

man pages are split up into 8 sections

① ② ③ ④ ⑤ ⑥ ⑦ ⑧

$ man 2 read

means "get me the man page for read from section 2".

There's both
→ a program called "read"
→ and a system call called "read"

so

$ man 1 read

gives you a different man page from

$ man 2 read

If you don't specify a section, man will look through all the sections & show the first one it finds.

man page sections

① programs
$ man grep
$ man ls

② system calls
$ man sendfile
$ man ptrace

③ C functions
$ man printf
$ man fopen

④ devices
$ man null
   for /dev/null docs

⑤ file formats
$ man sudoers
   for /etc/sudoers
$ man proc
   files in /proc !

⑥ games
not super useful.
$ man sl
   is my favourite
   from that section

⑦ miscellaneous
explains concepts!
$ man 7 pipe
$ man 7 symlink

⑧ sysadmin programs
$ man apt
$ man chroot